VOICES CAST OUT TO TALK US IN

Voices Cast Out

Poems by Ed Roberson

FOREWORD BY ANDREW WELSH

to Talk Us In

UNIVERSITY OF IOWA PRESS Ψ Iowa City

University of Iowa Press,

Iowa City 52242

Printed in the United States

of America

Design by Richard Hendel

The publication of this book was

supported by the generous assistance

of the University of Iowa Foundation.

Printed on acid-free paper

Library of Congress Cataloging-in-Publication Data

Roberson, Ed.

     Voices cast out to talk us in: poems / by

Ed Roberson; foreword by Andrew Welsh.

          p.   cm.

     ISBN 0-87745-510-4

     I. Title.

PS3568.O235V65   1995

811'.54 – dc20   95-1031

                                        CIP

ISBN-13 978-0-87745-510-3

For Lena. *The dedication is in the form and her friendships.*

And for Bob Supansic, John Seidman, and the Harmattan Group,

to whom I owe much,

> Peggy Bierer
>
> Kathy Boykowycz
>
> Catherine McCann
>
> Ken Roberson
>
> Cynthia Vanda
>
> Frank Walters
>
> Andy Welsh

CONTENTS

The Aerialist Narratives

A WAY IN

A dozen years ago or more, Ed Roberson presented me with a ceramic pot he had made. As pots go, it is solid and fairly squat, firm rather than fragile; with its ornate lid it stands about ten inches high. The outside surface is scored, and pot and lid are glazed the same: dark brown and light brown of mud and rock jostle each other with no design – rough, volcanic. But lift up the lid and look inside: a smooth, clear interior appears, a transparent blue hovering between turquoise and aquamarine, as deep and quietly beautiful as the sky of a calm spring day. Why, I wondered, did he put the earth outside and the sky inside? But several years later my one-year-old daughter, making her daily circuits on her father's arm around our home to visit the stations of things to look at and touch, knew that the pot was the right place, the only place, for keeping a special toy, her colorful and magical Jacob's ladder. Each day she would reach in and ceremoniously lift the toy from its blue-green home, watch the panels of Chinese paper unfold down one side and the other, then gaze into the empty pot before returning the ladder to its watery sky. Since then more years have passed. And now in this book I finally hear – in a poem both riddle and myth, in a voice already on its way to becoming another voice – the words for her wordless wonder,

> given to
> look into   the bowl
> of sky
>
> for it to fill
> with future . . .

This book is given – first to the poet's daughter, then to the rest of us – to look into, to wonder at, and to watch it fill with meaning. "Time does not finish a poem," wrote Jack Spicer. Ed Roberson's poems require time, and they will flourish through many rereadings. In contemporary American poetry there is enough, perhaps more than enough, of the single-voiced poem, the obsessive, confessional voice, say, or the windy, romantic voice. The voice – or rather, the lattice of voices – in Ed Roberson's poems is something very different, closer in some ways to the intricate language and complex beauty of medieval court poetry. It is highly technical poetry, in the sense that it uses technique to say what it has to say: the poetry is in the saying and is not something that has already been said, then put into verse.

The technique embraces all the dimensions of poetic language – diction, image, music. But especially fundamental to these poems is the idea of different voices using the same words to say different things. In the opening poems of "This Week's Concerts," the phrase "the perpetual jar of things" – plucked from some book of Eastern mysticism ("I don't know where / from") – unfolds like a Jacob's ladder into "the jarring of things," and "a jar of things," and "things ajar." Each is a motif for a different song. Another poem from the same section of the book watches a hawk (and other things) suspended in the air –

with so

little flight no one notices it

is predatory

– one voice lazily saying "no one notices it," another saying more ominously "no one notices it is predatory," while a third voice sounds the alarm: "It is predatory!" In "The Aerialist Narratives" there is another poem about flight: the flight of birds, made possible by the "nothingness" at the core of their bones, and the flight of nineteenth-century slaves northward across the Ohio River, made possible by the "nothingness" they must put at the core of their hearts. The "aerialist" narrator (who also is simply an aerial, picking up stations from all directions) hears the voice of an old song:

wash away your tears   tears   wash away

your tears   are the rivers and even they will

wash away

Embedded in the refrain of consolation ("wash away your tears") is a simple voice of hope ("tears [do] wash away"), then a more triumphant voice of hope ("your tears are the rivers and even they will wash away"), but also in the background a stern voice of eschatological prophecy ("the rivers . . . even they will wash away"). The poems of "Interval and Final Day's Concerts" lay out the basis of this counterpointing – in the figure, for example, of a phonograph needle on a record scratching out an ars poetica:

> Point in these words
> 　　　takes up the turning
> 　　　　　subject
> after the silence after
> 　　　　　　what was meant last.
> 　　At renewal.

And again in the following poem:

> 　　Where alternative interrupts alternative
>
> no idea lives long enough to see
> through and is barely music.

The invocation of music throughout the book is not gratuitous; the sounds of speech, the movements of syntax, and the rhythms of meaning become in these poems a complex musical art.

Music and image folded beautifully together in ways more familiar to lyric poetry are present as well, in abundance, in the sight, for example, of geese landing on a lake, who "come in motionless as seed / and make the surface bloom," or in a riddle-poem that sees a great blue heron as "a tablespoon / from wch the wings spill flying / slowly." And even a wrenching poem on the murder of Martin Luther King, Jr., the last poem of the book, is beautiful as it tells us of a recurring dream of sunlight and shadows on the balconies of America, a dream of trying to avert the murder by turning back a sundial as large as the nation, a dream known all the time to be hopeless and yet necessary to hold on to – "something . . . / or die away into the night lying."

The accomplishment of form appears in larger structures of the book as well: the elaborate reflecting of poems and voices by counterpoems running beneath them in the first half of the book, for example, and the architectural perspectives and transformations of the seen world created by the "up in the air" point of view of the second half. This is poetry that invites and handsomely entertains good criticism. It may be some time before its tapestry is completely unfolded, but that is happy work to anticipate. It probably will not come from the professionals of criticism, in university departments of literature; their attention is directed elsewhere. The amateurs, the lovers of poetry – who love language that is compressed and focused, at the very pitch of diamond precision even as it is unfolding like a large, showy rose – they are the ones who will map out for themselves the discoveries in these poems, just as those did who, for love, first followed the language of Whitman and Dickinson, of Stevens and Williams, into a new country.

"FAR HERE COME"

That country includes Pittsburgh, where Ed Roberson was born, raised, and educated, and also New Jersey, where he now lives. Because he has climbed mountains in the Andes and once was nearly killed by a flash flood in the mountain jungles of Ecuador, we glimpse in several poems orchids and foaming water fused in a landscape of fear. Because he has crossed the nation on a motorcycle, we see the dotted highway line rotate in the desert night and run up the sky as stars. Because he has worked in a public aquarium, caring for luminescent tropical fish and swimming with dolphins, the submarine realm of these poems is richly populated (notice the cormorants flying underwater). Because he has been a potter, the figure of a jar in the opening poems performs a complicated art of centering, and because he has been a night watchman in a warehouse, we see in the penultimate poem of the book three straight poplars and a burning bush appear in the warehouse aisles. (Interestingly, although he has been, and still is, a university professor and administrator, none of that experience seems to touch his poetry.) And because Ed Roberson is a father, the experience of caring for an infant daughter frames the poems of the first half of the book, the daughter giving her name to the dominant verse-form of those poems: "the lena," a form of interruption and shifted direction.

A new country, then, but not a foreign country. The bittersweet experience of an African American poet's life touches its every feature – the bitterness deep but not despairing, the sweetness savored. And yet, intertwined with the elaborate beauty of these poems, closely and cunningly worked into them, are voices of pain, pain grown too familiar, the voices speaking in modes that range from formal elegy and lament to gospel and blues. Most poets sooner or later tell of personal pain, when life comes to be chronicled more by losses small and large than by its gifts, and this poet does too. But we also hear of our national pain in these poems, the long, deep fracture lines of pain that run through the geology of American society, for which the African American writer is our keenest seismologist.

We hear of – we are not to forget – abducted Africans drowned on the middle passage, of slaves following the night sky's "drinking gourd" across the river to freedom, of lynching's strange fruit and of blood in the streets, of the killings of King in Memphis, prisoners at Attica, four little girls – four daughters singing jump-rope rhymes – blown apart in their church in Birmingham. We hear – we are allowed to hear – a stunned and bitter young voice just learning how things really are in his homeland:

> What your own
> people never wanted you to have to know
>
> and feel sorry for you if you don't

of the sense of betrayal taking up permanent residence:

> it tells us who we are we are betrayed

of one's inner life becoming "double minded" and of dissimulation becoming an unwanted routine in the manners of external life:

> my blood
>
> has had to lie in
> absorbing the lives
> we were losing.

And we hear of endurance, of strong hearts giving strength to others, of John Henry and of Moses – we hear a victory song:

> having stood on each other
> didn't we open the rock like our hearts
> didn't it bleed too to yield too to eat.

And further, almost unbelievably, with all "the bitterness of this fruit / clothing a nation," the aerialist narrator at times seems to see from one or another of his odd perspectives that all this is "illusion of separation," in which people, even good people, get caught. In "Ask for 'How High the Moon,'" an amazing tour de force near the end of the book – a poem that in midcourse begins to run backward – the whole moon half lighted and half darkened, an eerily beautiful jellyfish, sea and sky, snow and rock, the cycling seasons, Ella Fitzgerald, and a preacher in ecstasy all want to sing and to dance – with you, "the light and the shadow holding together." Our aerialist sees, I think, not only the past; he sees the bowl of the future, too. Filling. Oh, look. . . .

Lucid Interval as Integral Music

THE FORM

Picking Up the Tune, the Universe and Planets

this form is the lena
after my daughter
here she is I will have to
hold   on a minute tell you her line.

a scribble
the universe and planets holes and scribbles
pure
interruption she gets   her changing

she is the only music   she gives
the intervals
in which it is written.
she is

back she only wanted me to pick her up to say so.

---

1. still autonomic
still as

1. still autonomic
        still as unspeeched as conception's
            about what now-breathed message
reflection prior to its face
        should carry you
                        at seeing,

about what you claim as
        – If I am the lake you take your face from –
a reflection
at the sight of me,
                    I crawled

as far back in as I could to you
        into the water's trouble,

        into yet templet noise
            between each word,
inchoate sea that spirals as shell does out
        – helpless as any later meanings –
as the world.
                    The father has

always been brought to his knees
        by this.

fear that
the terror the peter pulled out short of

bearing, always tricked, had this
time also got through,

that twin, the disorder, stowaway again,
had, with won life, reset all's possible end,

and that fathers, held to more than
their power   songs now cover,

have to re-face
        meaninglessness,

clutching infants who
        haven't yet words,

screaming for them
            their protective songs
        incoherently.

THIS WEEK'S CONCERTS

I.

because the final
confessions of a coarse air
bail the fire out
we are innocent of adduction.

taking the body down
we thought was a solo for fuel.
shoving it in for warmth
we cracked

our perpetual jar of things
to a more
naked jarring blast.
the crimes wch you wear my body for

I myself committed.

II.

songs without words
scenes of infants.
or o sing unto the lord
good morning as birds.

tribute to the saintly
the bait   the killers.
endangered animals
will they survive? this is all.

the perpetual jar of things
i don't know where
from   it's caused   or filled
or quoted without these words

I am shaken.

---

2. I might have screamed
        the wrong spell, the wrong words,
    the wrong defiance thrown the property
        against the specie for,
    for love
        written a senseless draft and wasted
    myself at war, like my age,
        remembering the more complete
    for bottoming out of means
        human
    to even sit down and eat beside another
        to ride on a bus or go to school
    to recall any chance at all of an even
        hand   free of the holding
                                        class

III.

the   rice care
is left in the frog harp.
several early songs
hurt the farmers' heart

after nightfall.
to mention the soldiers
is to state it to death.
a souvenir silence.

string in a labyrinth.
no giving away
is the look out
commanding the entire face

floating without bottom in that earth

---

remembering the more complete
        the more the perpetual
jar of things
        lends no aright,   nor tapped,
no center on the wheel. all form, all voice
        is clay. in different. we
are right only
        to what we give birth to, anyhow,
we are correct only within
        what we create,
only
        the examinations we make
up out of each
        last hour's erasures mark us right.

IV.

The park geese
are dozing at their dance
on water.
Their necks

in the straps of their closed wings
They are swung like subway riders.
depicting the floating
carcass

is a high form of held
Instant in dance
As fleet as death is in life.
the river stone is here

A black step in a tree reflection skipped still.

---

4.   because of the suggestion all the versions
         of peoples in trees make
to americans,
      the africans, the pater monkey, the
        jesuses crucified, the lynchings
the yearbook blondes swung in
     all the alumni arbors,

the surface of the water reflects what is
     Under the umbrella of such leaves
        Even stone leaps to the surface
The stones on the bottom are mistaken for the bottom
    of a hanging
       black man's feet on the surface
reflection. Dancing nationally in the trees or.
     A skipping stone. also skipped still   strange fruit

V.

A sudden smoothness like a glass
between the swells   enchanted valley
wandering the wild sea drifts.
The cloud deer cross the road,

the main shipping lanes,
searching after it   in the snow
it is that master
flake of all possible design

when compared in size.   the pin
of the spin of the ocean.
of all migration
The course of the target

only   makes all the objects.

---

5.   You can stand in a field at night and hear the snows land.
    The ton of an instant's impacts taken all but one,

    and a sea cleared in silence for that's star:
    and seas of the mirror moon

    that radiant from, say, one crater
    taxiing to time as copernicus.

    That flake.
    That sound.

    The beacons, the landing lights strike me as spinal,
    as physical shivers

    the silence in which this traffic fields
    its tar baby.

VI.

there are no stars in
the metropolitan
area skies
only air traffic.

twenty-one landing
lights. call
that mobile
the constellation Holding

Pattern. a modern
form in time
enough to save our navigation
of a maintained

in the nebulaic   escape of bearing from here.

VII.

With the dead rest
spots in the oscillation
an accuracy also,
a perfect note is

hit. An accurate physical absence.
The presence of music.
Or conversation
with one

I think is never missing
and I think is the right signature.
to have squandered an intelligence
on unspeakable watch

of that   without tongue

VIII.

the cobra standing
drops down to strike
like   the tabled elbow rolls the arm
down to the mark of the hand.

on the stairs
of the snake's crooked back
the fangs hang out
on the landing.

whoever's on the floor tonight
his chin on the concrete
will spot their scale as the last
conscious credential handed out

not any manipulation near to a signature.

In mesoamerica the snake's head touches
        down to the ground. You are bitten
            by birth. It isn't a trick.
You start
        dying. How can anything kill
            you ascending the steps
to the hour-
        fanned feathers of skies?

Our pyramid   is we've perfected
        not being caught,
throwing folk skyward through the stories
        of structures absently
as hope, elevators we prescribe in the voice
        of those who stand watching

IX.

we can run out of our side
streets like out our ribs
between the buildings of owner
abandoned meat   to see the dead star.

we can bleed as really as
humanly possible   and prove nothing,
raise no more of the dead than good has
in our lifetimes.   lying in the streets

are stars   while their perfect point in shining
on the books without meaning to be fixed upon.
secrets   which orbit decent decision
so distant from anywhere   real

seeing to it it is only in our stars

X.

blood: someone says it's not
red until it runs
up and touches the air
loose.

it probably has the light
on different
inside and can cross on the knife
suddenly appearing through

appearances not even as particular as street.
the thought of.   the light changes
passing through limitations
like human skin: candlelight thru fingers or yellow

vision the distress symptom of rattlesnake bite.

XI.

The fast storm sky   wiped so suddenly
clear the stars shocked open
enough   the Lights went grabbing clothes and
screaming   The bore cloud white as the moon

a totally vertical moving aperture
was taking off up into open noctilucence
the head boiling   Then the eye
passed and the storm laid straight into us

what it is like
in cliff dwelling is in the ceiling.
and the view out from under
the seal of the earth   as an assurance

that this edge is sharply into air and that breathtaken

XII.

the walls become whole,
you can throw away –
to live for longer periods without
– the packing boxes,

and you can keep
a few things too large to move quickly;
the floor is level, they won't lean
in that vortex down at you.

you can feel in the danger the danger
down a little turn achieving a vacuum
that seems to emit what world as falls in
as passing out of you   but this is only where

it's gone   there is no afford of measure.

XIII.

the builders baled chambers
with dry wall and stacked them
in the fields. the parquet
of contour

farming's planting
is taken to a wall
the shot hung
for aesthetic record.

the refugee fact
is that this is peace.
those who are its belongings
are stripped

ballrooms turned into body shops

XIV.

I pull a curtain of the great cats
around me   I am singing
a nightsong in the siege of their forests
raining on me

I've washed up human
& it is no good to me this hand
does not play but folds
at the heart   not beating

the dark
spades in the meticulous thought
of fire. The were-freedom
the joker once beast and part man

votes part nigger on   the cleanness of choice

---

14. about august, burning almost
    black with the heated green,
    the closer you get to the flaming autumn
    the more silently white

    iced you are getting. roughly,
    the closer you get to something the more something
    else it becomes, we say.
    it's always something, you say.

    People conceded, OK
    you are exactly the same as I am, good
    at this, maybe not at that. like me, OK
    then sold and moved out of themselves.

    those ghosts are as constant as season in the U.S.

XV. The Local/Elevations

or if the lips ever actually moved.
or in the middle of
an ambidextrous carpenter's
move   if the benchmark

is on him or his work
the loose foot of the cauldron?
allowed to join   repairs   the union.
or if the deadliness of this new health

can bottom this crashing out.
or something?
imagine a unity   even without even one
never-changing leg to stand on.

or if the new man's thickened lip, healed, fixed their remove.

---

15. I resort to the mantle of my one free
vote   and out from beneath any win
it may cast   flies as from the eagle shadow
the mousey possibility of any

loyalty from the opposition.
its retreat has been backward through right and
wrong, philosophy, through god, through common
decency of individual man,

to founding and contract law, through fields
over rivers, down streets, through the finest
schools, infinitely transformational
against color   like some gene of camouflage,

profound deceit rather than local hate.

XVI. No

The rocks have lines waiting
in them.   The fielded conduct
of turn   crusts
into the municipal

A geologic result.
finish after finish
woven into a carpet like track
stubs by times.

Not a patient design.
Most of our movement
forward has been laid off
The wire moves   its stratagems.

The lines in rocks only move mined   against brokerage.

---

16. and all the while the ordinary
    white citizen is realizing
    what the sabotaging
    indifference to the achievements of the black
    citizen means
    to them   the evidence of the war
    kept coming in.
    some indifference to them.
    The words never regained their arrangement
    After then
    Everything had to be doubleminded
    like the nigger had
    had to do.

XVII.

a carnival of bald deer
their antlers lodged
in the walls as the forests
of heaven

for the angels who never leave the grounds
of the hotel.
the skins on the thrones
in the lobbies.   ensconcionist

this litter's one   with the least
hope   this runt of everything
letting the property escape
escape the ruins of its solemn occasion. o

then is this thing already over

---

17. after having moved out of themselves
they probably moved into hope

hope has the least of everything   no stores no
you have as much of nothing

of them in the afterimage
they leave   as they have

they return to buy back
in in the coin of other image

concerns   having lost
the understanding   , as hope, of least

XVIII.

the rule of the spirits guesses.
our rules   tear holes with firmness.
the water is a girl in algiers
a blue robe the nature of thirst.

the final tableau of her waist
is seven studies of clay fish
the dampened color of unglazed pottery
ascending as lark

– like evaporation.
sister. I see your face is pale.
it isn't funny how your dark skin
is capable,   that unfinished leak

that lazarus   water   is unsweetened

XIX.

the fireworks mariner
took a quartet of winds.
sleeping everywhere at once
lay beauty.

the scarab he had swallowed
he would go inside
as blue secret.
if she were under the container of the sky

he would simply kiss her everywhere.
the straws of the unfinished
sun basket
the activities of living weave

to a small opening   the moon.   her inside

XX.

you have to run forward
and touch the terror of the offered
hallucination of light that packages
what life

you're going to get kicked
back from the voltage
you'll live.
I know some electrocuted

people who are fields
blown like the sun
on swaying configuration
of spaces   their body holding

their fires out to you   as what was charged.

---

20. Things that take a few blocks
       to stop   move across the street   Bridge or no

    One of the stories I'm most afraid of steps off
    the platform two steps

    ahead of the Metroliner.   I thought it was me.
    All express has no longer the reason to

    whistle   Among us,
    right of way is sufficient address.

    I'd thought   that as music I should
    wait for the listener   But you know

    blues give a museum   to no reason to and waiting

XXI.

Their body holding
Their lines like their fires out
To you
as what was charged making

The field.   They draw hot
attention hotter and hotter to
their cold eye.   at the face
the storm on the empty

makes   brilliant afterimages collect
of the disappeared
into inside   into nothing
known

And that is what they say.

XXII.

I walk nights
in the falling gardens off
the edge of the flat earth
theory

I observe jump
as the sentence in a
step (that ditch
plunged that flood-future tops

as endless spheres cannot)
turning
always up ahead. I work out
true in the disproved

information I will break in the morning

---

22. The enigma chambers are poses
cats put their bodies in and walk away

Their tongues play that fur, that dark
profane harp, about our hands

My hands pour not being able,
like salt   if sea quit its solution

Dances table like water in the ground
We call it a journey   a map

cats put their bodies in and walk away
They tear into pieces   The wonder is finer and finer

musicians   The black cats

XXIII.

sometime I'm going to have to
explain how I feel how
I've made my peace with lives
of the waters

how working in a public
aquarium night shifts alone
years
after the last high ground in the flash

flood in the amazon
after the orchids   saved my life.
I have been stared at   crying publicly
remembering   crossing the street. Now a bird

of an infant dream asks for just such a hand over

---

had given blue feet to police siren such
that I thought the scream a jazz jade bowl and a step

And I get over
So severe a moment of border

was that character of black life moment
to moment

that taking it to the bridge which means that's it/
to jump   was at a twelve-lane standstill

Even our screams cannot move
Cats put their bodies in and walk away undroppt.

XXIV.

As a boy there were no black boy
scouts   as a man I hadn't learned
the contexts made any differences
in the danger

and I was dumb
at the waters signing away the boulders
rising   as I was used to
my father's business deals making him lost

in thought – behind his sly manners –
of us and our love of bicycles.
we covered that town like latitude
lines on a map crossing his warnings

like neighborhoods' color   lines like him

This to the bridge music is our art of. period.
What surrounds or rather ghettoes all immediate point – i.e.

rivers and all that edges
off into loss –   dance bridges,

a stepping over in the mid air that is
mid music.   Dances tabled like water there are clouds

We drown in your dance, fathers,
not in the cold waters bordering separating

land from land
where we wept when we remembered

XXV.

and now here I was in the amazon
headwaters calmly rising to run
at what is like a shot that is
the only consistency of sound)   being fired

down   from high in the office
scale gullies high on the mountain and building
titanist echoing run-offs   into a drowning out
of this heat in the ground up route I was

breaking   moving on   up this lower canyon
too far
and too frightening and the only
place on earth

for us who employ ourselves to the map of this world

The river hid the land   so we know
it hid us on the edges also at night.

I wasn't where you end and I begin
I was all over discrimination

like jordan was some north fork from some cross
country nonstop flight: I couldn't see it

I know this country's race-catches by our heart
but I didn't know the faces.   The catchers.

You would think I had known   this
too is the side of a river   these few blocks NJ

this land is salt
built up of the sediment of your black tears

XXVI.

it is a flash   flood
and we're going to drown and we ran
ahead of the first rush and the slower rising
into the night until trapped   in the lightning

we slept four men in two bags. I haven't said
anything about the wall of the orchids
inside the water
-fall off the floor of the jungle

two hundred feet
overhead or how I took the hand
of fish   reaching into my stomach
and made peace

all I have said. And dived for the public   aquarium 4 to 12

---

26. The step, within itself   isn't difficult;
    a lake, at one point,
    of understandable stillness,   at full.

The footprint on the water, filling.

Often you don't even notice the steps,
that is that each
is bridged by the falling body to the next,

discontinuous though the ground.

XXVII. Huge Spaces Apart We Still Look Each Other Face to Face (Santa Barbara)

I had three people tell me
that day   they saw me return
down the canyon as a hawk
I saw the same bird the same

time I saw the blue of the
sky straight through the open
shadow-work on the mountains
I lay in   the golden fit

of mescaline sunning naked
on a rock overhang
above the canyon thinking
I have walked back to before

we left the earth

---

what are the flock that always lift down
into their shadow's valleys
out of the cloud of those bodies

but your step?

The settlement of grace locates from street to street,
takes the subway, flies through the air.
Black children jumping within the doubling wombed

wave propagations: double-dutch.

XXVIII.

when I saw it I thought I was hundreds
of centuries ago, and just this much a
this here and that there thing
is what goes on ago. form's clothes are

the dust on my nakedness   I can draw them on
with my finger through it
on myself   I can look at the hawk
and be that much drawn it as here

and that is what we saw
as one of us.
something never leaves us no matter
who walks up the canyon or   what

civilization or shape we leave the earth & the others for.

Often you don't even notice
              the end   the great way ended;
the steps up the sky   taken
              apart for construction
                    materials;
though a tile of the floor
              in each our houses resound
like split reward,
              some advantages you can't cover.
you use
              but some exchanges of change
throw plasma
              fields over the fields over
for former slaves so   no ghost or equation explains
Birmingham : Church : Double-dutch : Window : a new rose
walls off the ends of your buildings.

XXIX.

the variations on god
save their invention
for its human face.
the cornered dances

of the mouth confess
the antique ikonical rose
on its lips
had a day as cannabis

in the illuminated margins
where the specie arch-literacy
divines the daily
and common for the ritual light

to be given   though as the rose Window, a match.

                              In the end, in the darkness,
        in the smoke of the sent off messages
        of candles and even finally bombs,   you don't expect
        – framed in the same venereal oval as mary's clothes,

        except that theirs are simply two jump ropes –

        four little girls; you don't expect four little black kids
        to be lifted by a powder, by a speck like earth,
        into the steps   your government takes,

                        jumps. Blood rope.

At Any of the Bethabaras: Metempsychosis

they come in lives   within doves within
lights within   again and again cycles
to sit on   their own shoulders in one
life   the innocent's and the corrupting's.

they bring trouble upon themselves
like the spotless mirror
lake in the country brings down wild geese
in its season   or in the city

the statue of glory its common pigeons. Such rains.
they hurry the stain through   its entity event
laminae   to the cleansing free
of its hollow.   the infinite heart

of it all washed away

XXX. Red Shift

The summer drift's evening
submits a bid
on a list scene.
It catches. and moves

into the breakdown
accompanying a huge
purchase
A monstrous seat of value

in a sunset
Is taken off the truck.
A look at that size
vision   fugitives landowners

who'd moved here to get away from colored.

---

30. They make the day follow the night
    out of themselves
    Children going to sleep by jumping
    up and down in bed   knowing they fly
    Their shirts   their nightdresses fill up
    with their song   sometimes the cotton sack
    itself for clouds
    they headed for the clouds   go home   and be free.
    You have to believe you breathe
    every black breath ever into you
    it takes you   the song
    Says I'm gone   I'm gone   oh long, I'm gone.
    The bottoms of my feet   those are clouds
    on a dark   long-legged sky

XXXI.

influence it
was strayed very far
we misrepresent if
we place

a coarser sensibility
soft light and delicate texture
compounded of mist and light
slight shifts of color.

in subtlety of generation
time to qualify
as an antagonist
safely removed leading

a certain monotony in seeing

XXXII.

We had seen a first
Lady haul ass
over the trunk of
the assassination car

faster than split
second's
photography could catch. it
Looking for the spirit

leaving the body
We find character.
acting to refer
our scramble over our dead

to a common class. not exactly a pietà position
on all fours, bookin'

XXXIII.

Information
planted on event like dope
to jail a cause
of this or effect that This

Doesn't get the connection.
Meaning-set
is less than we have mind for.
Leaving stuff

not booked through state parity,
that can't be thrown
into change for correction.
Asymmetry   is the already   in the happen

of character to making   a representation

XXXIV.

one of the things we were
We were supposed to work for
and we would never see
like real gain or character

until disaster
Mixed what it pleased   we have.
to stand for
from the beginning

One of the things we were.
was never there
but at an accident of moment with
Us   and that never with us

is never added to to add

---

34. – never added to to add: moment that cannot be worked.

To the extent that our senses have moment
meaning is fragment.

The way we can leave   this time
the photograph

is what before   left us
the definitions of spirit and soul.

The questions of what was behind
the mirrors

the photographs answer
when we put them down and go about

XXXV.

something stretched out on balance
rocks overhead   with so
little flight no one notices it
is predatory except

the shadow-reading
audience   which as supply could care less
if that need's majesty
is endangered in its act.

high orders,
almost culturally flightless,
unable to lift us.   the currency
of exchange between is madness's

equipoise   in camouflage   people as air pocket

Seizure by Simple Error

probably some anatomist knows why:
such violence is usually warning,
the result of which unheeding is taken
to them to study by taking apart.

the misjudgment of space rings the elbow;
the taken out of you blinds from the solar
plexus; the taken between the legs doubles
males into a place they almost reach

again in their female, the foetal pose
in the mummy wrappings of muscles in pain.
and the point where is touched off the massive
shock of the body is as shrinking

from autopsy as reaches of heart or spirit
or judgment destroyed in all even motion if hit.

XXXVI.

It is without example
It has no steps yet it is about the heel
As the brevity of sparrows
Or as tho elevators were stacks of dimension

of where stop goes
now flying across the present floor
so many leaves
of a paper on   the whirlwind this flowering

grip of an explosion
lifted into years arranged in the vase collar
of your shirt
from one mine

you thought a seed & stepped into the ground
and your head goes off

XXXVII.

The notebooks are where the foot
soldiers are buried beneath
where the war is won.
A lot of this mind

is the flower yard you will have
to go down among and find
gone.
You are not kept up either.

Grave out of which inspiration were
to raise
your figure is cast on that very field
ground reverse and lives are opinion

changes which do not occur in space.

XXXVIII.

in this song the people are singing
the parts of the wolves.
the last seven stones to say
yes it is the moon and turn blue.

the dances of abusage have a sequence.
the taller and shorter addresses
of the skyscrapers on the avenues
of the misery   on music. notation.

but it's the elevators who're anonymous.
whose wings regard the earn and the cross fictions
as as early as wax
and ringing ears in sophistication

of screw in this aural flight at suns turned out.

XXXIX.

A T-square regular
milky way
horizon
of interstate

headlights
cutting the desert
in its distance
from its night   sky

moved the wolves' memory
some ninety degrees:
"So   this is the moon
Again   When I was dust

and this was in the making it was these dots."

XL. I Have Opened Six of Ti's Nine Knots

There was a piece of brown material
out on the table.
I try everything against my skin
for whether it wears

right with my color   people.
I had bought string.
a weight up to six pounds
its horizon. its power

by powers would be
increased by the knots. a fetish
making about to release its mysterious actual
on vision   vodun

has sent me nine ships   in a tie-dye rag.

XLI.

the puzzle in bundles
is change.
you pit it together
it is one thing

(contracted in the tying   rite of casting
a material over the head of
a space   knotting it
with strings as it   escapes into

the shrivelled cloth
offer it to the   colors
open its horns & tentacles & it is another

I am   tied up with my skin somehow

---

41. this is about songs
        about when they happen about
        pieces and absences
        of connection about for no reason

        this is about practicing
        any gap any short for the jump
        this is about going about
        years with the live fragment

        singing it over
        and over for years learning its meaning
        only as accuracy   not an aesthetic
        only as the most

        maybe empirically correct song

XLII.

there is a cleft brain talking diamond.
it is carbon.   something
has burned.
I am unmixed about it.

something is brilliant.
at opposite purities   shit dealt uncut
the fixed facets' cool smashed   the blinding reflection
the one in the other darkness

remember the do rag
that held a process together tied
on the head? the two piece
bundle   dealing

harder and more expensive white quiet

XLIII. Simbi Petro Damballah La Flambeau

this volcano is the univalve
sea creature's structure
I forget the name
it rests on

boarding the unseen language
for the profane place
this creature rides on its licking up
its location. this univalve is this volcano

who ties up the land with new earth
with its hot tongue   coldbloodedly.
the sea shall unwrap
from around the stiff bone of the lost

on the middle passage   an ejaculant fetish layer:

---

43. To the extent that our senses have moment
meaning is fragment.

The way we can leave this time
the photograph

is what before left us
the definitions of spirit and soul.

the questions of what was behind
the mirrors

the photographs answer
when we put them down and go about

XLIV. The Seven Deltas of Shango's Wives

wrapping the land in new earth,
wrap me in your arms.
winding down a sediment
out of deaths   for flower, settle me out

under your layer
for every inch I'm worth   deep
knot.
I have come   unloosened

from a chromosome division   reknotted
to print in the standard of days   my days unfurled
from that tie of the umbilical   unpicked.
Now   from tied deep in you by the flesh   river seed

lay me down fanned out the mouth new manned   land

XLV.

where day   sun's long pile
for hair
casts the knot's   divination
wear dey a dreadnought for hair.

in the head a matter   is tied
that unpicked   clothes time.
given nought light so for see through
wear dey dreadness far hair.

day monkey eye
come open now.
who no know go know.
where day ah dreadness?

far here come

46. after having eaten the rice and beans   alone,
one piece of rice

after the dishes are gone
is the size.   not the weight.

the sound crumbs of the sea
that the delicate

reason   comes down to
feed on,

from the beaks that are clear of meaning to,
are brought back up into

the umbilicate ear
out of the seizures of the organ tides,

out of the breaks.
out of the storm, the jazz.

INTERVAL AND FINAL DAY'S CONCERTS

Interval

When the plane crashed I was snatched
fast at the navel until I hung
from the seat belt   and then I laughed.
Birth snatches you one life to another.

dislocating as death is the upset
the move to bethlehem means birth is,
is the apple-burst,
the turning birth unthreading eden a bite again.

The midwife calls it the apple: My daughter's head
snatches my life out of me into my father's towards me
to her. We laugh.   Snatched by biology's cords,
by lines, by responsibility's leash and my tail's urge,

I've been around.   dislocating a little from each by each

I. 12.b.obs.OED

suppose you read in
say like law   or history   The New York Times's
This Week's Concerts
in aural rorschach.   carmina burana then

and caramel burr insectivorous sweet of light occurs.
moths and anti-crime light. and how you feel about leaving
a three-month-old unattended   keeping your hand in
this short   an interval, a current fixture.

the out of place-ment, the come up short cut-paste, the edges.
the abruptness so familiar now as to be
fluency from next to
next becomes

1.13 suppose to read is as to study   divination.

II. Isolating the Nurturent Reflex to Sound

a picture an idea a question transfixed in the short
of interruption   strobe
rhythms that an infant's limitations   period by need.
inextinguishable variation   on forgotten

rite that five hundred miles inland and out
of signal range read and wondered
what a pacific two-thirty-one must sound like.
perhaps november steps.

or that all these stops that pull you up short short each
a different synapse
means   the current crossing takes up moment outside
as in lena and that different place   incompletes   fragments

Chance is specie our daughter our mind

III.

knowing the music
        never comes into
                it.
the music's fact is
        a glossolalia
            sound's meaning.

record jacket
        -cover art's point
              cuts its own
        music
different from that
        the magnetic pick-up
              fit is on.

Point in these words
        takes up the turning
            subject
after the silence after
        what was meant last.
    At renewal.
A needle
        not so played on meaning
           as on moving
rescue   from blank death
        death's and other words' subject
              radical.
    As many names
for the same deck as games,
      as human call is
        figurature
upon those acids.
           And once in person,

IV.

labyrinth is a real route,
densest in the middle of the floor.
there most crowded with loud intents,
and deepest from any door.

going in circles would be the same but for
that's being at closure. the stillness and the turn
on repetition is missed here
head-on without the recourse to driving pattern,

to memory. Sense becomes the multiple spot
of collision. phosphene spiders, talk as
variable as the trembled focus makes face.
echo.   Where alternative interrupts alternative

no idea lives long enough to see
through and is barely music

V. Photograph: The House of the Poet

I see the house of the poet,
weird and quiet, right in its out of place, across
a wheeling field come off some wind's cart
that tilts up into fury's trees above the house

and think   a black man ought to have such
signs in his cross-
roads taken pictured too   landmark status:
a small writing desk   in a quiet corner

won deep in the mass of no less subject
than white tree worshippers of paper
their cannibalist sacrifices
flipping through them   offered that order

be maintained white   where his ink darkened those sheets

VI. . . . Apart from What Each Other Is . . .

you can see goethe's desk
beethoven's piano freud's couch.
my brother can show you my father's best ring,
and I can   my mother's, my grandmother's

vase on top of my manuscript closet.
and I had wanted . . .
My desk: I had wanted every black grandchild's vase
to be taken on on

that desk and that desk stay in our hands
like a plow singing hold on hold on.
Silently brightening your corner . . .
But we are sold

goods   apart from each other

VII.

the fairy tales were over   and had grown
explanations   and had lit connections
to sense   like pubic hair.   torches.
but she had grown huge

breasts she does not want
except to stand up wide legged
to the toilet and fist them out
until they're dry and free. her brain a clear

mammillary structure   crypt and dry.
she wants to take up what's her from endings more
recent than seas and earth. the nerves' story
that start is not upon once, and time can take up

anytime.   and body   any story from any cover.

VIII.

They say when
off the solid
ground of all nowhere
a chill steps

into shaking   that bog of nerve
-tangle the back
muscles like mosses fire
in   (the ignis fatuus

through low spore clouds)
that someone has just
walked across your grave.
Whole armies have swept back and forth

across this trigger hair of property this year

IX.

Ours is a foolish fire
we bring you
into   , children. The light
clouded with all these each others' weather

of that fire itself   weathered
safely or not. ultimately not. The light, you see,
is of kind, is
of way   Ours is a foolish fire   done

out into air   with mirrors even still going out.
I look
like my father you look like me My father
ashes over in his lungs colder to cancer

I heard him say god how I love them to us under his breath

Whose sleeves
is an opening that became a kind

Like it   dividing and indifferent blue
could be a kind of poem like blues a music

We count too few returns capable of
being kept time,

other patterns of recurrences than mathematick
of being capacity.

The clouds so few they would rattle
around in   the count on   your one hand

The increment like fingers
Here   hold this

But whose sleeve
doesn't have   a hand in this. Jesus wept

X.

That everything can go

(Simple change)
And wrong not so singular
nor infrequent a stop
that you could commute by heart

the line from sentence   capital
birth to death period.
Just   Right   :   Straight time deliverance
carries the structural sentence.   Everything.

As hearings, the voice takes these unequalled stands
against an odds immense as sky like this were air.
What is this?   What is the air   after?
Only audience and cry leaving? Then everything goes?

The Aerialist Narratives

CHAPTER ONE

I. Aerialist Narrative

Written into   the drip accomplished
form   of action painting   the lyric
for people who walk on strings

There are photos of people standing
on the canvas
in mid-air   a line ahead of the painting.

Of what happens,
lines of that   are gone,
not simply missing

Those lines of how those
lines that are there   got there
the line in mid-air

from the can to the surface
its moment like a line written
in that falling hand of the northern lights.

But what can anyone have read,
supposing it was night,
by the light of Icarus or any of us escaping?

II. Taking the Print

See night in the sunlight's starry reflection
off the water   darkening the water
by contrast.
                    The dark hiding in the water
also hid us in the river at night
Our crossing guided by the internal sight
on our darkness
                    the ancient graphis
and – from this passage of abductions and escapes –
this newer imprimatur of the river
cut deep in the plate.
                    see in the river the ripples'
picture on the surface of the wind the lifting of the image
has taken at the deeper face
                    the starry freedom
written in the milky rivery line that pours
the brilliance of that image from a depth only black
night fleeing across this land
                              has to voice.

III. Heading: The Landing

The beacon fires,   the hidden fears;
the runway lights,   their nature's lies,
the country's lies:

will arrival even be any
base left to touch
once these few minutes run out
their approach?

Is a way in air   so clear and orderly
as the light is,
drawn as a landing about the ground?

Voice closest to closure of the journeying
is one that deserts us,   the one called silence,
leaning in the glass against its image,
as if all diagram is a delusion of process.

All these voices come out to meet us in this
ancient seeing in the end of distances
this fearing:
the glow of the coming city
on the horizon   is it burning;
is this music or screaming
all these voices cast out to talk us in?

What if in the final
minutes of your heavying
descending

the landing strip kept lying
changing you back
into the air   the way a white

backs away in anger when you approach with the directions
you've been asked?

In like manner the entire society remains
up in the air   black unaffirmed mirage
a mountainous range   teetering on its own
                    upside down
        peak denying what it's risen of.

Solid rock lifting itself into the air
on its own heated reflection   illusions of separation
                    that anyone trying
        to place down   to integrate into   goes also up
                    in the confusion.

Ours is a particularly hard landing always
trying to correct to an abandoned position
        You run out of the fuel for holding
                    back

        the fires of arrival

the few survivors
            those who packed to die
            maybe raised

            like images
        of smoke
slapping our faces with our color

a wafer from the stack
        of all our waiting number

            a cup snatched
        before the take too much
                    to

        A kind of conclusion
    that's cleared away.   Like wreck or sin.

IV. Waterfowl Landing: It Lifts to Close
(for Ron)

The hundred wings float down the furrowed air
to the lake,   come in motionless as seed
and make the surface bloom
that way
that drops of fattened summer rain
open against the pavement
tulips' petals
like wings lift to close on landing

V. Properties

After some days –
    and not because of the dirt –
it really looked
    like a kind of earth
and not the fallen sky it had been at first
    snow.

Whether the vengeful one
    were the ground or the sun –
then,   whether thats
    stamp or kiss were a crash or press
into that print
    an attempt coins on survival,

– commemorative myth,
    the spun tales of these genes –
whatever,   ours, like water's,
    is not material fatigue.
Up and down time after time
    how many migrations
has ice made home
    to water?

The verdant tropical mists' drip
    tears   gathering into the cold
bloody rivers of the atlantic
    grinding ashore
captured into the plantations' white glacial field
    the rending melt water's burst
toward a north star   state to state
    of matter

pressed upon us
    our material does not fail
the strict coinage   It would be different
    if the investigation team had overlooked
a piece of the wreckage in the staring face
    of Icarus

Black with the roads' dusts,
    the atmosphere,   solid, on the ground
turns into a pool, the
    ground's mirror,
and picks up the sky again.

VI. Cape Journal: At Sand Pile

1

    it matters less
than as long as
    their shapes last

    that you call this
a cloud   that a whitecap;
    and less

    than either, this
answering   a name
    yours   mine or

    the how many names
of snow: flat, shifty, six-faced
    cold
         families   of New Jersey

2

I felt,
    for less than a wave
        washing over, why
the hermit life heals,
    talking together
        after so many years.

This morning, walking alone,
    fortunate guest walking
        the blank beach,
I remembered
– because I had listened   to both of us –
I'd had nothing to tell.

And that   is to say, thankfully,
Paul, I also have no memory of Rutgers.

3

the wind erasures
on the dunes,
polished unlike our
confused images

these removals are the composition
clearing
the principle of composition

the sand clearing the water by the end
    of the wave
the caps clearing the horizontal
    water into the air   a moment

and contained as in the glass ball of that moment   the coast
and its raining afternoon
and the waves in a fog of dune grass here

4

    No one had yet left any steps
in the sand, no old suggestion
    of limit as

    to my own locomotion.
I could be flying.
    – though only in this direction.

The return would make this clearer,
    put it on the ground,
    put it to measure, a step

like music   This should explain
    a feeling of being fortunate   more
    than just the beating out the distance one

in front of the other.

5

simply because we have forward
facing us
in which we see these things

6

the beach grain
by grain moving   the length,
walking the length of itself

7

Robison Robinson
Roberson Robertson
Robeson what does it matter?

none of the crackers
keeping records
on us could spell, either.

I am clear.
the length of myself I have moved
the melanin color to color

8

so when daddy decided
to open his business
by filing according
to white people's spelling

none of his brothers had any
of the same
names
stupid crackers

everyone remembered them
telling you shut up
you couldn't spell
hell with it then

look in my goddamn face
and see
my damn name

VII. African Ascendancy

ascendant an ancient
    use
for ancestor

mine ancestor is
    seen upon my skin
a light that color is

    upon the surface

mine is an African
    ascendancy in sight
at sight   a burn

If yours were
    the eye of the sky
what would the source

    be of

your look upon me,
    what would it grow,
what would its color be?

    How do you burn?

VIII. Research at the Interstice

This is the Sargasso Sea
where the mile kelp is the muscle fiber
of a body so huge   we are,
in this hull, at the membrane of cell exchange,

we can pass as just overboard
into another stream,
carried as riches
to the new world.

Up above my head

the dripping sky
and the rising deposit-built wave
that the darks disappeared
from the light down

into   from their shore
into a cave   a hold
carried treasure
We could surface from   as from a wall

deeper and richer than memory
the marble carries of surf
the netted fractures the spittle
of froth   We are only running

nitrogen fixation experiments
a sample of each depth
in a glass ball flask
off the North American Coast's

former slave states
to see what the light
reaching into the dark sea
has made of this

IX. The Motorcycle Crossing

1

Sometime it's all in
　　how you get seated
　　　　in the road of the morning   This morning

I was sitting right
　　at the desk kicking out
　　　　paper like miles

and like coming up over the top of a hill
　　into sun   or air   or clear
　　　　of the high road roar

I laid her over right there.

2

You don't think   you run over them
　　and snakes can rope up
　　　　into your spokes
and throw the bike.

　　It takes nothing,   a stone.
　　　　So ain't nothin happenin
in the office   and you lay it down
　　mean it
　　　　all going down inside.

Secretary step in   you
　　sitting at the desk   unannounced a
　　　　silver veil of tear weaving down

your face   a landscape
　　singing quiet to yourself
　　　　Every little thing
Gonna be alright.

No snake   no slick   no stone
I just laid it down.

3

        Late afternoon summer
the long rhythm of soft running
        water and its silence,
            you could hear the wake of the collards
parting the water.
        The long black lines,
            her fingers,   passing through.

When we were growing up   you know
        those sisters at the sink
            in the kitchens   baptizing those greens
suddenly break
        down into tears   jump up singing
            shout
Don't worry
        Don't worry   some day
            It a be alright

4

must be in my blood
        blood my blood

            has had to lie in
absorbing the lives
        we were losing   bathing in screams

            The tide rhythm blood
and filth took on
        rocking in that deluge
            those ships cupped to our god for drink
must be in my blood

Given our own blood to drink
            Bloods of the hold
Bloods of the fields
        drying in those furrows
                through our feet

as up through any root
        blossoming at the tip
                of our touch into the cloud
boll   held an instant then sacked
        the bitterness of this fruit
                clothing a nation

leaving for work this morning
        in new blood   a new press
                the rungs on the upward ladder
treacherous
        as the deepened sea.

X. The Comb

The water,
clean, beached and pressed
and laid out in a pool

like for a sunday
the church in the water
the morning   holds.

The morning pulls
through things
Seaweed comes out in the comb of black bone

The morning picks up a shiny black stone
greased shining with simple water
A day of redemption whatever its word, its name.

Out of the kinky tangle of waves
the small, balled curl of a pool,
small quiet huckleberry of a pool.

Someone screamed, "Land!"
When we looked at the horizon everyone wept.
We had crossed this as though it were a drop
                    from our forehead

No more than a ferry commute across
an urban river   but in mind a toss
dreamed at the hand of thy neighbor making news

chasing a kid into traffic
as his offer of that other shore   his aim
for you

XI. Given Way
(to Tom Mellers)

Flying isn't always that best
    you can do left
behind, that over and above
    spoken of.

Sometime you have to return over
    the river as the limo driver
      after having

seen off a burden of chastening
    envies from JFK,
      have to,

though driving, passenger a sleek
    abandonment,
and lightened to nothing of your claims
    have to

drop your gloves as though a will
    from the wheel,
drop the rein that points the way less
    than the barn itself, the throttle

less than place in tight formation
    taking us on in
               flying

Not that transcendence, not a grace;
    though, like it,
no choice, an automatic
    pilot

how it follows the road has brought
    us to the bridge
on the fly of crossing and not
    the stop of jumpstreet
off.

And if,
as you say, Jessye Norman   was singing
    Jerusalem
at that instant and the structure

    of the bridge,   in crossing,
painted trusses of Franz Kline blackouts
    on   the lighted city,

    flying is only
how you've seen what you had to
    stand on
and not had way
            to look.

CHAPTER TWO

I. mblemati.txt

We don't associate
                            arrows with flying
anymore.   For us,   with guns,
                     they point.
They gauge
                 they speak the distillation
– that direction –
                        of once flying.
They haven't returned,   in a sense,
                 to earth.
We are the flash instead
                that precipitates from flight.
Even most birds
             are a dead issue.

We don't take the road
                 as a way, but as door
for its shortness.
             For us with our elevators
to make of our horizontal
            basis   concurrent
spaces,
           the road is, at most, standing
in line to be through.
                     As door to our next,
the road keeps glazing
               titles of changing entrance,
such that now when we think of life   it is
       as standing before a huge time or directional sign.

II.

stepping through I
mean getting on a train
plane a subway one place
sitting down
getting off someplace else is
so natural a sequence
of positions to us
we forget their addition

that step   choreo
graphically speaking   could not have
possibly arrived us at
this location alone I
mean we dance
but in formations   in steps
partnered to sequences left
outside

I mean gaps like natural
limitation having
stepped across because
not snakes   we fall from step
to step finitely forward
towards that end of ourself always at
our fingertip type limitation
we run out of   breath at

each word   said
then not said   there is that
Then there is this   created limit
not what is hidden by that us as
horizon   but what we hide
with eyes open inside   out
of sight   what we deny not the unknown
but the willfully not

            knowing   that
is stepped over because less
intestine than we are shits
we step over
pieces we leave out
of the trail strung to sing our
histories what has come of
peoples we have eaten we
      no longer see
      We have eaten we

III. Heron Riddle Flashback

I   **answer**

Summer and three quarters
    of an hour past seven
        in the evening

But I could tell what it
    was by the silhouette
        I knew the answer

to this shape   great heron

    a blue passing over
        these garden apartments
            from the lakes

of one corporate campus
    to another along
        US 1

2   **heron**

    the first one
I'd ever seen   you showed me
    at Pymatuning in
        Pennsylvania
about   seven one morning
    after
        we drove   –Catherine, you, me–
after tripping
    to see   one of these beauties

    the neck
        poured back upon
            the bowl,   the body;
    the legs extended
        after,   the air-
            handle;

a tablespoon
from wch the wings spill flying
slowly,
a heron.

3   **silhouette**

time also is only a riddle
Of shape   as in how we try
to animate the frames, the takes,
the shot we are given
how we try
to piece to life,
between dying   and that concluded
out of only meaning,
a master   if only of tape

Mistaking for this sequence
of pieces   that whole of water
in the river   where ever crossed,
lacking that started finish
to journey (in which all that lifts
must land) of gravity,
what is it . . .   The silhouette   of the bug
helicopter collects
behind the spoon

in the folds in the lattice
of meanings that a wing stirs
the overlay fixes
one of a combinant of likenesses wch each
manifoldly persist   beyond
its analogous moment   miscreant   chimerical
Stilled heron whose next instant   is head throbbing
thunder   chopped into beats   a medal music,
whose white is blue is an unseeable

green   whirls its wings   around above its head
       speaks in blank concussion-
              bomb balloons   the dust updraft
like wing curls down   the floated spoon
       calmly lifting through   a dragonfly
              the swamp mist   northern pennsylvania
What is it   imagery of   any longer
       to have pushed these defiances we popped
              the smoke   the brilliant buttons
opened   the flowers   what is it

       when craziness you saw far off as
              human gets   is in line   in succession
to office,   not a distance you had stretched
       atrocity,   not a vet's disability you see in,
              but tried   guilty   and pardoned business
What is it   collecting behind
       the files collected on
              everybody   and still the bankrolling
the agents   left outside to kill
       little bird-leg children
              going against the background to church.

4   US 1

They told us
this shit would come back
to destroy us

       now how the proudly guilty are ashamed
       we were the innocents, the paranoiacs

       embarrassed we made only sense and not
       some something more unseen than the violence

       openly whitewashed with the public face
       of government   against us

              they told us
              this shit would come back

5

    where the commuter copter gets confused
with the heron   with the rotation state

    side   the bombing that the beat carries
out at the crux of Jimi Hendrix   with

    the Princeton corridor air traffic
shuttling the white boys into office
    Audubon collections

on the wall   indistinguishable

    from a reserve   vintage privately flown in
and a reserve   US helicopter on weekend
    maneuvers   a cocaine spoon a dragonfly a heron

government   heroin flying in   proven   on the wall
    and you'd suppose   not to be confused

the wanted   with the stamp

6   **riddle**

    I got your letter
    It didn't make a lot of sense
    Are you alright

    Nothing escaped you no
    abandoned you yes nothing
    abandoned you   that's it

    You only pretended it was
    imagination
    easier than to say your eyes were open

We know there is
something
that is not an image

that we
turned quickly enough
and could see   with us

IV.

      The skipping stone stays out of the water
The standing up in the boat crossing
the delaware,
the band-aid commercial parade
of drum, flag and fife,   the iwo jima
collection,   things that are terms like
four little girls flying

      around inside an exploding church,   people
being washed down
the street with water,
dogs in the saint george and the dragon
art history position
on command on top of women
the camera catches,   the skipping stone

      stays out of the water
long enough to cross over
concurrence   to accountable term
but not over   the deaths of those who go
under   say just prior the altared shore
who are entire now.   complete, not ideal.

      A prediction of that bird iridescence,
the spot of a single reptilian scale,
is passed without going the full length,
to one down the sequence   suddenly
across the looped catastrophic
plane of locomotion.

      Tossed off on blank sand,
the line   in a sidewinder's hand
explaining lifting off the continuum
of the earth,   explaining leaving one surface
for another   to arrive elsewhere
on the first   in time

to take up the percussion of living
on the one hand and have to
strike death into its dance down the other,
any distance between   coiled tightly
around the rattling emptiness   to drive a sense
like that gourd's hidden singing   of beaten time

    from inside   secret   singing
to fly the round walled ground the seeds throw
like bones   the steps   our coiling hips
our music   leaping off
this plain like light a dance
that forward takes us higher

    How if stepping skips those places,
how then dancing flies.   how
matter admitted and explained lifts from its lie
its term of flight accountable to be done
something with   a stone touched down to resurrect
prediction to a dictate
to organize our missing   and from that ghost create

    those backs of the waters
we cross upon.   those black shadows no
that black apotheosis
in the simplest shared indigenous american things.
already.   an Osiris
the middle passage has brought home along
what rivers deltas and mississippis mean to U.S.

    But this is what is always skipped
this is the lift the country gets to get
moving   the term
mickey mouse renewed each generation
evokes your hugs   What face stirs your concern
like one of color except   to lemming separation, to out-
       distance
       is renewed

V. Cinquain de Lune

Why do you think the moon is lying?
What has it said
That you've found otherwise?
Is it that white?   Is it that
White?

VI. What the Return of the Lines Meant

We only move in close
    on strangers' backs,
we make primate approach
    only on line
        anywhere near
what all our senses are what all
    our like's perceptors are
        about.

And all those whites
    who'd never darkened any line
opened to light through blacks
    fall in behind
        the shadows,   back
like their fathers don't admit
    is where he got his
        first,

    is where he stood
when lightness pulled him out
    of turn
ahead
    as the official course
        of things aparted.
Now it's all back   hard time
    in line again   and not together
        not familiars this time either.

VII. Chorus at Ohiopyle
(to John Seidman)

The trees on the other side of the rapids didn't
impart the peace we'd set off our escape for
They all leaned to one side like kids in the back
seat pretending to take a fast curve

only it was the wind   Or it was the track
the eye rode on the waves that, when it got off, slipped
into the ocean   that illusion   the land
no longer still nor solid   the borders laughing

Or too much dope   Or promised lands awash
in the tangled rivers of that wider water,
everything crossed over and the landing here
that sharpened our fixes 'til we see displacement

bend tree to tree the agitation of direction
smearing away all settlement and peace.

. . . Always going someplace
else getting out of what we'd found
ourselves in that too horrible
we were always what we had
to change if you weren't
you died jumping out of boats
running onto points of iron arms
landing unsirened even longer under limbs
of trees growing up free base wild
enough to throw open the carbonous streets
cities of the hardest material.

So we have forward facing us   the trees
on the other bank of the rivers
point in their rapids betraying any line to.

We were the point
        that was our trust in our line
was our lining so beautifully the pockets   for

what   was the line of our dancers
    that missing this point sold us
out   of each our cycle

west
    what is this emptiness not one
this plural not   mandala

    I have to step in
here I have to skip something   stop
    here to tell you   voice by voice

point in the line of thought   in the sentence   the poem
to the extent it tells us who we are we are betrayed.

As much as cost as geological
location as space marked out for play
the proximity of people not me built
my house   where I'm at   what I am within
distance to do my culture what I pick up
to say back is set up by how far apart
I keep from a subject just this kind of thing
keeps persistent   I elect reps who say back
that isn't so and hold out
a hand with nothing at my end I'm bound to hold to
the line I draw I draw back to what drew
up the ship and my position on it
I don't understand why I'm sold into line
    – I had a contract –   headed for these skids

From where the rocks were now   I could look
to where   they had moved from,   I could see
the formation of the canyon   a whole

face shearing from the wall   dropping in steps
we switchbacked down as road, ledges we trailed
down into the river   scree   lapping its own pile into

structure, slide outraced by its cloud   pendent motes of
slab   terrace gardens   behind the front running
boulder breaking the ribbon of the course

of the river   where I sit in a wave
shaped in the rock to a seat by water
I can see the falling into place

and I am riding it
all afternoon   boulder mid-flight its skip

I get up   walk the aisle of the valley
come back to my seat   ride some more
I walk up to the head of the rapids –
On my back,   feet first,   I paddle into
my seat   in the rapids   my ride on the flood

Instant the catch of the current snaps me in
in the motion I hear all this laughing
rioting in the flow but voicing softer
than the hiss under the roar   of light
bubbles tuned taut at the molecular

level   traces of ancient dissolution
lost   african   all these bodies in the one
body that is water we go over
dip after dip under   thrown back up laughing.

All the lines we have lost seem to have come
to stand in this line   are these the reunited
spirits riding the amusement of this park

on hailing waves of hands all prodigal
brightly names balloon up to the surface
a hushing sound above it all   being tapped

or is it a twitch of muscle   on the shoulder
from the cold of the water   given
some grander answer by death   you can't hear

above the rapids   They are here
not the windy lake wherein
but just as grand not

They are at the molecular level
Not at our amusement.   At home

VIII. Gnosis

Not that it's one of your own
staff   your own people lying   against you,
but that the cramped hold is within you
now   always an edge

Not just the rough day,
not the whips of the weather, the overthrow
of the waters against you,
but the anything

you can't take   it
has the condition of the ships, the fields,
the escape
now,

you think about it,
you can feel the mornings we would lose you.

IX.

           The birds put inside
      what the walking felt divide
          their going,

      what   – without that void,
          the ground between step –
      brings walking to its cul-de-sac.

      The birds put nothing in their bones

In their bones
    how nothing frees them   how nothing lifts

them up   What your own
    people never wanted you to have to know

and feel sorry for you if you don't
    takes you to the river told you

wash away your tears   tears   wash away
    your tears   are the rivers and even they will

wash away

I was afraid
    I find out what it mean
                it a be alright

what it mean what it   meano
    mean   it mean
                it won't   no and it won't

matter   at some point
    even that
                be alright

                    the right
                    build in

their bones
how nothing frees them
how nothing lifts them up
The birds put nothing in their bones.

X. Elegy for a White Cock
(after Mei Yao-ch'en, ca. 1002 – 1060)

With suburban real estate rising

anywhere it's snug up
    the butt of the rural,

the roosters who used to

make all those promises
    are fewer and fewer.

        Lifters of the dark, nightblooming labia,
        Comers of the light,   et cetera.

Any birds you can call are less.
    Call them   messengers or angels,

flight or ring announcers in the laddered wrestling

up through dumbness . . .
    Our deepest carriers   in specie planes

go down, blow up   like birds nor angels never

        could admit,   get hijacked . . .
        And the unit

of the morning, measure of temples,

how could it
    matter to a plumb-line fired by we   unfeathered

that in its infancy cracks an orbit whip

off Jupiter's
    huge head?   matter

        to this shining semblance we
        spot in a glide for setting

down,   eastern's early coach at dawn,
        our morning star?

that silent cock of the spectrum,

up   at our changed limit . . .
        Our fires once our horizons.   Now out past stars,

what started as the simple reds of roosters.

* *

        But
        There is no one   from this apartment   who you'd expect
                to hear morning   chanticleerly   with any sense
                        since wake-up radio   and traffic
                                reports
                        abruptly shortened as by the neck
                        by live transmission of one crash
        into the Hudson off 44th   some mechanism loosely acting
                                your fox.

        But that is gone too that red too. Some tale of water closing
                about it, white as ice   because,   in a moment
                        the last attention failed.   Everything
                                got across
                        that water in its brief window as footing
                        but the loss at   the end, the end of the red
        tail touched down with cold white.   Like black blood is
        in the western light   where it touched the sea.

* *

old farmer, poor as dirt, maybe older even than dirt is,
surely older than these kind of stories,

had a rooster got to be his pet, his friend . . one night
he hear it holler, something had done snatch it . .

he run outside to chase whatever . . he end up saying, "who
could use cinnamon and ginger on him now?" that exactly

that exactly where we at.

* *

Our wolf at our door   or earlier
          our cave entrance   or closer in such distances
of time to us   just outside our fires,

a wolf of minute just night's side of ebb,
          those barely eyes twice the morning star as cold
and more unmoved than heavens were ever wished,
          fixes a hunger into blue hairs
                    and disappears in this direction
                              as a day.

The cock crow which rules   that night hungers have eaten
          all that earth has turned
up,   the meaning of wolves   dissolving already
          into light, the quick of foxes'
                    fire just so much flesh, so much material
                              of suns,

                    recalls the sides into position.
                              That exactly where we at.

Where,   as that call goes down, every revenge, each justice
          unreturned by then to the balance
                    we thought we made as a fire,   it dawns
each scheme again that these are periods not any
          understandable score
                    of resolution we can study;

where,   around a fire we thought would keep the fox
          the wolf the chaos off
                    like the timekeeper crowing on our side,

we sit with loss, the unreturned or absence for timekeeper
and only the summary embering to study before,
far on the burning horizon, foreign pictoglyphs

begin arriving written in the broken dazzling.

* *

You could wake up with the set still on,
still in the process of drawing
the pictureless, blue brightness from the dark
through the antenna   it seems

until,   too much,   a clot of day hangs there.
Vacuumed tightly to the teats of the antenna,
a blue static backs up from the little window
into day,   pressure after frameless pressure,

emptiness after emptiness.
Halting,   in that counter-telescopic
squeal of static,   our star
entropies into place

among the waves,   the blue echoic waves
that thin and feral lips of the event horizons
pull upon and break along
a spectral line like shore at sea at dawn

clear as the line of the antenna is
the perch for birds
to finish the extension of their wing
come down to this

* *

Birds are taken in through the t.v. antenna
to the screen. Only the squawks of pain

and the shout of eyes in the darkness against
some fox of broadcast.

Some favorite and antique hope is silenced.
                              . . . You lose your damn rooster,
we lose our commons' farm to suburban imageries,
then lose our images to speculation in returns on anomie.

The land, the vane, its bird who names the sun up, lost
in a traffic of the windshield's focus, lost, the morning
star,
                    the very morning itself.

What spices could you use on this death
when it   in every pot   is tuned empty

an iron bell in your stomach spooned against?

See how the thinned blood day uprises
hungry over the hills in reply.

XI. Onze

Not birds touching down,
no petals falling.

The sharpened stars are
throwing weapons,
metal cold.

Moon, disintegrated in light,
countless escape ships of invasion

land its image
on each branch, each lawn,
all the roads

closed.   Snow.

CHAPTER THREE

I.

A widow suckling
    the master's field,
        bent over the rows,
the oddly backward

    trajectory of the bolls
        of milk
she runs with her hands,
    the cotton spilt

        from one breast on the ground
she fingers each drop
    into the sack plumping beneath
        her other.

Up on black mountain
    a child will spit in your face.

II.

bomb
bullet

        trajectory is only a line
someone has to draw it

or pull it out
and into the papery fibers

of skin,   the responsive
skin   where the slightest
initial mark,

the silvery slip of a kiss, the trail
writ of a stick, a whip, the ink
dip,

        sets up the conditions
of the art

living the line
drawing,   dowsing a delineation of
the human

so I thought the
silver lining was the inside
of a cloud
that flashed like that

little leg she shows when she sits down
her robe opens   across the plains of the bed

it is the outlining
of light

around the edge of that dark
cloud between her legs instead

and the inside of a cloud

that slicks with mist the divination
tools of beings mostly water
briefly written

III. On the Line

People die on the phone

Severe thunderstorms of guns

Snubnosed   silverplated

the lining on the ground positioning
    the body

        the cloud   the written
        something about how to contain
        a cloud

        how to carry air without a wrapping
        of leaves   of houses torn
        from their foundations   loose papers

        the spring arrivals of smells
        gliding song
        birds

the city in a basket   the jewels
of its lights in plastic
bags used
to house any evidence

Lanes are contained within the yellow line

The yellow line of the sun   the broad daylight mark

Wave-length maps out the colors

A city that chases itself into traffic   death
    escaping a band

    of the spectrum
    a black body erased across the tarm someone
    with a ball of mason's chalk recalls

into an outline on the night ground
uncoiled, the breath drops its wrapping
the target that was skin   the arrows

the flights
the beautiful
cloud

The potent balls
of his eyes   turned off,
the whites turned up,
are bagged.

*

Too sharp to look directly at   (not the brilliant lining out
          of cloud form against background   but
The line drawn through us   (a different
          marking off of   conclusion   We are looking at
Struck by lightning
          on hold   writhing in the news
waiting on the open connection with extinction   for news
          of help

a call connected at the moment
of birth
in nonsense and over time

what adheres to that screaming
is language torn off
a background   a neighborhood shot up

our single mother
a speaking color
a cloud

of event wrappings
dropped into those plastics of form
that the moving line around   one holding the chalk
picks as evidence off the closed ground   of the other.

*

Rain

IV.

There were these
mistakes between   the steps'
walk continuum   and the reign

of the consequences
of absence bam a lack
lapping misstep   that break
the fall of

a man into rising from
a crash
land or the skip   free

of the takeoff   Seemingly spontaneous
power to lift off
to change   is deep   as religious

transformation as off
the water
the stone   the moon
the bird of spirit

flashes   People
do suddenly lift into the sky suddenly open
Not in this state

*

Punishment was supposed
to teach society
(teach "them" society)
But the teacher taught only
punishment
And when the punished suddenly

had learned

The change here was not achieved
by punishment's
format, not by the teachers
or any agents of punishment, but by
the punished
themselves, by those supposed

lacking.

When what is professed to be lacking
was achieved,
when that responsibility,
that manhood, which rehabilitation
for once had actually achieved,
occurred,

state troopers were brought in and shot them.

*

There must be
space between the trajectories
of the rain

of police machine gun bullets
that could trace the shape of a man
escaped
into more than smoke

from these
attempts to stand for
some kind of decency in living

even if it is come to
within
the meditation upon mistake

some country
the citizens of attica
had learned to re-think for all of us
and expected

rather than the barrel
that the nation
stood around the rim of
shooting into

them

V.

And O
When I fell down on the ground
When I opened my eyes
   standing over me
      the light of a long freight bearing down on me
      around his face   one of the gandy dancers
      hitting a lick of the horizon's flying rail
      organizing a whip into a riding   he opens
      a place in line for me
      lifted in the physics of that singing
      rail   I am
   looking down at me
I lay down
When I opened my eyes
   standing over me
      their floated forms burned to invisible
      black bodies hiding stars   they lie
      the ropes of phosphorescent nebulae
      around their necks   moving like tie
      beams slatting the black night
      sky into which   from earth I hang
   looking down at me
I lay down
When I opened my eyes
   standing over me
      that start star

      trail slicked with the bloody
      feet of stealing themselves

      a way
   looking down at me
I lay down
When I opened my eyes
   standing over me
      one of the road gang in
      chain seen or unseen
      each his hair a rocky ore that burns
      into iron that splits the stone
      that splits iron chain into fires of spark

flying free   I am become
         not just one of them but that one
      looking down at me
I lay down
When I opened my eyes
      they were rock under my feet
            I lay down
            my road

                              *

when we made the middle passage didn't we
walk the waters didn't we
have the waters paved with the skulls
of our grief for each other didn't we make it
on ourselves.
when we crawled under the mason dixon
didn't we jump the fence over jordan
didn't the river re-bed behind us and
turned blood because the bloods wouldn't tell
didn't we make it to this one side on our other.
on ourselves didn't we
get put up when we went back down
home didn't we hide in each other   no hotels
that we stood   uppity   a chance of gettin
shot didn't we walk
on the shadow years later of emmett children who did
didn't it make your step
higher than just to walk.
didn't the westward push opening
the country turn middle passage trying to shut
us out panicked at the plow flat and hardness
of our feet having stood on each other
didn't we open the rock like our hearts
didn't it bleed too to yield too to eat

didn't it

didn't it didn't it rain
didn't it rain

VI. Handed the Rain

given to
look into   the bowl
of sky

for it to fill
with future
see it turned

upside down on the grass
see the ladle pass

hear the god underneath
calling his inside
the heavenly vault   eternal

how that bump
reminds me   how we saw it
once

from the underside of
Nut   a mother's belly

see dissolve
against her vast ground
the drowned cloud of black

lives   the solution's population
of rain crowding the city
in the belly

see it now as the sea extended
the drowned city   lit   in this sky

see our sky
the bone clouds casting
African

tomorrows   only
an arm   black balletic cloud
extends itself

dark nimbic
invertebrate squall

I am handed rain
by a portuguese man-o-war
These are

new skies
once we absorb the seas'
solution as the bodies lost

the sting
fire of lightning   flesh

the water
body
air

we drown together
in our living
to drink

from this
bone

VII.

the flock of black cormorants flying
    underwater   are these the songs returning
      the escaped   lifting down into the cloud
of current turning
    back out of the fields of coral bolls
      to the abyssal skies
the undercurrent home
    to this day
      noticed   off any shore
the pile post   the cormorants alight
    on   Legba's mark
      open their wings and point

the bodies shining in their feathers

VIII. Ask for "How High the Moon"
(for Nathaniel Mackey)

     a half moon at midday,
if you've seen
    the gelatinous medusa

you know how it looks
   like it leans
its jelly umbrella and melt off-fringes
    into the wave   and wind
       of sunlight

The organism's membranous
    delicacy, a silk stinging
      thing like beauty
carried above beauty   carried away
   the sky its

      pale parasol borealis
the bride a gauzed nubian shadow
      moon holding   carried away
damask balloon torn in two
   over itself.

      Such as yourself,
        say,
     living down to what

      means
the melt pools in the market lot reflecting

      a sky
   the ended days of freeze
have glaciered liquid flawless

     can afford
    for looking up . . .
     Leaving the store

I overheard somebody say
　　"Look,　the full moon,"
　　　　　　at only the half

carried away up.
　　　And down time after time,
　　　　　how many migrations
has ice made home
　　　to water?　and winters, to this spring?

the light and shadow holding together.

*

　　　　　　　　If in
　　　　the very pool you're looking
　　　down into to look up　　at the moon
　　　　　　　out of　out of
　　　it is thrown at you　　a stone
　　　　　　　from the tire
　　　　　of a car plowing through it
　　　　　　　the turning

　　　　　seasons' wheel　Or
　　　　　　there appeared
　　　　on your forehead
　　　this stone that backwards
　　　threw down　　into the water's trouble

　　of turning and tire　that arrow
　　　　of time which film reverses
　　　　　stilling the waters Then
see the hard thought at the bottom
　　weighting the reflection of its moon
　　　　　creation　　loss
each distinguished from our ghosts

*

Sculpted out of the sun-polished snow
the small david of a puddle

out of how stones can sling up at you
if you're looking   (arrowheads   the moon

ignescent associations between things:
the cold star struck from the broad day.   Light.

When Ailey set it
to music Billie got knocked down to

what a little moonlight can do
the white stuff of cost

danced   to music ask
for How High the Moon   and you want

Ella to sing it   bring it down
like that time she admits   carried away in time

she can't remember the words to this
but what she does in time

is
greater song the rest us

jus mostly cries out
no forward no back

                    *

hit in the head by the moon
no one can take the stone of that light

out of your human skull
no one can tell

where the bone and the sight
actually separate
                    now
the lost sight of all gap
opening on that

nothing they put in   their bones

                    *

the light at midway up
        out of the darkness
                orpheus

all you persephones   you lazari
        christians and other
                resurrectionists

is that circle of listening
        decided
                to tear you apart

I mean this song
        this stone wants
                to dance with you

IX. After the De-Tonations on the Moon by NASA
(for Bob Supansic)

We choose that others mean
    something ourselves amass around
        in known receptors' shape
            But not what's said
We don't know.

Dancers have feet
    but the amputee can sway secret
        for secret the occasion
           of sound to place
a place that isn't there.

A step.
    That the air would accept us
        that the air would accept
           our song with its accents
of the ground and bring up the moon

in reply   introduces us
    into the touch that's kept
        But not what's said
          "The moon rang like a bell."
We heard and neither we nor the air were there

to speak that in its light of tongue
    but we put ours against the ice
        absence
           like the clapper   kissed it
and we stuck to words.

X. Ha

        I'm the night
-watchman today they call security

guards. All the same. They didn't find me screaming,
nobody picked me off

my knees, nobody had to peel my fingers free
of anything   about this night

in the morning.

        I leave the same entry, though,
that people have always said these things about.

like all good watch,
whether you punch out and walk off

or have to be rocked in a listener's arms –
floorboard by floorboard across this chamber – out,

like all good watch,

      the entry is unchanged.

         · · ·

in mind between three main
pipes against a reticulated gray

sky   the concrete block wall
the leaf flutter of an inspection tag

you have three straight poplars
deep in the far end of the warehouse aisle.

you would   expect the night
man to have lived there alone all his shift.

But this is the night turn you pull when you can't hold
anything else.

Things happen.

water is   as by straws
sucked up a tree by evaporation

off leaves   the vacuum of
reach for the sun   of change in state into

something lighter than blue.
We're as water   and up through atmospheres

and off the earth we water
it   seen free-fall   spherical tree that taught us.

you would expect   our burning
minds to trip gardens and falls like sprinklers.

This is the bush.

so its speech was cast print:
Grinnell Sprinkler Systems   the local grove

those who go live anchorite in the woods of minimum
wage hear their careers'

ghosts approach out of;
the sudden appearance of trees that plain

answers put on like night-watch issue   clothes.
As for this tongue of solitary, this's the bush it speaks

Deep in the far end of the warehouse aisle
as down some arm in the cluster called the local group

the Bell Labs listen to a bowl against the wall
of time   to next to no time going off

from the beginning

. . .

at the molecular level
time goes forwards and backwards at ease
or rather
the difference doesn't exist or matter

at this level.   at ours
we see the justice of the stars,
the balance in the arrivals of the seasons,
as if on time

−and they aren't−   were something to see of itself.
and we see ourselves as such,
an order,   simply because we have forward
facing us

in which we see these things.

XI. In Light of Dream

the American is a peculiar light
since then   the dark
extending from its balconies
really is

the country's shadow diving
out of the way
writhing to get King out of the line of fire
of that sun's sight

across the face
of buildings   coast to coast

a dial trying
to set back that weight

. . . something . . .
or die away into the night lying.

THE IOWA POETRY PRIZE WINNERS

1987
Elton Glaser, *Tropical Depressions*
Michael Pettit, *Cardinal Points*

1988
Bill Knott, *Outremer*
Mary Ruefle, *The Adamant*

1989
Conrad Hilberry, *Sorting the Smoke*
Terese Svoboda, *Laughing Africa*

1993
Tom Andrews, *The Hemophiliac's Motorcycle*
Michael Heffernan, *Love's Answer*
John Wood, *In Primary Light*

1994
James McKean, *Tree of Heaven*
Bin Ramke, *Massacre of the Innocents*
Ed Roberson, *Voices Cast Out to Talk Us In*

THE EDWIN FORD PIPER POETRY AWARD WINNERS

1990
Philip Dacey, *Night Shift at the Crucifix Factory*
Lynda Hull, *Star Ledger*

1991
Greg Pape, *Sunflower Facing the Sun*
Walter Pavlich, *Running near the End of the World*

1992
Lola Haskins, *Hunger*
Katherine Soniat, *A Shared Life*